# Passion For Life, Reason To Live

by

R. Lee Walker

Bloomington, IN     Milton Keynes, UK

*AuthorHouse™*
*1663 Liberty Drive, Suite 200*
*Bloomington, IN 47403*
*www.authorhouse.com*
*Phone: 1-800-839-8640*

*This collection is a work based on personal experience and personal convictions. Names, characters, places and incidents either are products of the author's imagination or are used fictitiously. Any resemblance to actual events, locales, or persons, living or dead is entirely coincidental.*

*©2011 R. Lee Walker. All rights reserved.*

*No part of this book may be reproduced, stored in a retrieval system, or transmitted by any means without the written permission of the author.*

*First published by AuthorHouse 02/23/2011*

*ISBN: 978-1-4259-5279-2 (sc)*
*ISBN: 978-1-4343-4356-7 (hc)*

*Library of Congress Control Number: 2006907215*


*Printed in the United States of America*
*Bloomington, Indiana*

*This book is printed on acid-free paper.*

# Preface

*Passion for Life, Reason to Live* is the follow-up to *Paprika: Versions of Wisdom*. The book contains poems and stories that I heard over the years from acquaintances. What I've written is designed to entertain you and inspire you. Perhaps the stories will help you be better, healthier, more loving, and more prosperous. Be a better person by knowing how to treat others. Be a healthier person by making better choices. And become a prosperous person by improving your judgment.

I know my book makes some strong statements and a few emphatic judgments on issues that are sensitive to everyone. Nothing in the messages is a qualified diagnosis for everybody's personal problems but suggestions to consider based on the big picture and the symptoms of those who feel isolated or worthless at times. I won the war over procrastination, low self-esteem and confusion about my purpose.

The most touching story in the Bible to me is about one king. He possessed a peaceful kingdom. He reformed the justice system, ensuring its fairness for everyone. Then he heard that three larger kingdoms conspired to take over his land. He only had a few soldiers and women with children to ward off such an attack. The king submitted to God because he did not know what to do. The king had faith and went to battle anyway, but when he got there his enemies had destroyed themselves. God fought his battle. Believe in God and your purpose.

This book is for you. I hope you enjoy my message of encouragement and hope.

In loving service,

R. Lee Walker

# SPIRITUAL ANSWER

The Golden Rule is how we are supposed to treat one another. We've been at odds with this consciousness, still not realizing that we should love one another and we are our brother's keeper. Seek first the kingdom of heaven and all things will be added to you. (KJV)

*R. Lee Walker*

# PRIORITIES

Your priorities should be having a closer relationship with God. Even if you don't believe in God, how about a closer relationship with the spirit of purpose within yourself.

*Passion For Life, Reason To Live*

# GOD GIVES YOU...

Enough happiness to keep you sweet. Enough trails to keep you strong. Enough sorrows to keep you human. Enough hope to keep you happy. Enough failure to keep you humble.

*R. Lee Walker*

# ROOTS

Don't just let anybody do your hair. Your hair is part of your moral and self-esteem. When your hair is not right, then you won't feel right. Everybody's hand is not blessed; some people have dead hands and if they touch your hair, all of it will fall out. Don't go back to them; find someone else, or do your own hair until your find another stylist.

# Peace of Mind

A great man named Anwand Sardot once said, "To have peace of mind, buy a house somewhere you can afford to live and pay it off, and then buy yourself a nice grave site. For as long as you live you will always have a sense of belonging and peace of mind"

# MAKE THE RIGHT CHOICE

All it takes is the wrong choice at the right time to disrupt everything. Adam and Eve disrupted the world where God had to send Jesus to straighten it out. Wrong choices at the right time can kill everybody on the airplane, car or bus. Wrong choices at the right time can make or break a million-dollar deal or destroy a relationship.

# SERVANT

I'm just your servant because I want to bring out the best in you. In doing this, I make the world a better place for you, me, my children, everyone. How do you serve? Do you serve yourself or do you serve the world around you? Who have you served today?

# Inspiration

There was a little boy that was deaf in his left ear. He heard that when you do for others you help yourself When Christmas time came, he brought a compass for a friend and he was not looking for a gift in return. In the evening he went over to his friend's house when he was not there to leave the present. While leaving, he ran into an electric fence and burned his face, leaving marks on his skin. His mother said, "Isn't it a damned shame? He got hurt trying to help somebody?" But while his face was healing, his hearing returned.

# THE FLAME

A sick woman experienced a burning beneath her feet and the pain would not go away. One day a friend came by and asked her if there was anyone she had mistreated. She replied, "Yes, my neighbor. Yesterday I cursed him out for no reason but because I wanted to."

Her friend told her to apologize to him and she did. A week later she passed quietly in her sleep. What warning signs are you getting?

# FIND YOUR PURPOSE AGAIN

When you find your purpose, you find yourself. Remember your purpose is located inside of your personal dream, which is God's calling for you. Your purpose lives in your dream for yourself. You might say my dream is to play the piano but I can't play. My dream is to sail a boat but I can't sail. My dream is to build a building and I don't know anything about construction. Your job is to help someone do what they want to accomplish in line with your dream. If you can't be the star help create the star. Both roles are equally important.

# Why Do I Keep Choosing the Wrong Man?

If you don't wait on God, you will always choose the wrong man. You must practice patience. If you are choosing the wrong man, then he is choosing the wrong woman. Send that married man back to his wife if you want to be blessed. When you know that you are on the wrong track you need to start asking yourself some questions. Why am I really doing this? How does it make me feel? If you're not glowing inside with certainty and joy, then stop doing it.

# BUILD THE SPIRIT

In today's times, people flock to vitamins, health spas and personal trainers, infomercials and magazines. People are living longer and healthier lives. However, they forget to strengthen their spirit, the most important component inside the flesh. Older people look twenty years younger but what are their minds caught up in? How are they nourished? Soon, people in their eighties will be running around with glowing, fit bodies... the old women sticking out and the old men sticking up. Without a mind they won't know what they have and how to use it.

Build your mind and spirit. Know where you are and what you really have.

# Escape

A small girl sat by the edge of a flower bed with an old woman. The girl revealed a tiny bird in the palm of her hand. Then she taunted the woman, "Guess what hand the bird is in," as she cupped the bird behind her back. "If you choose the wrong hand, the bird will die." The woman gasped.

"That is purely evil, you being in charge of that little creature's fate. No matter what hand I choose, the bird will die. You cannot command that power. You just want to use me as a scapegoat to justify your wrongdoing."

# Less is More in the Working World

A very long time ago when I first graduated from college I was fortunate to land two high-paying jobs. One lasted for three years and the other almost four. Eventually I got laid off from both because of downsizing. Most of my friends at that time would tout, "If a job doesn't pay what I *was* making, I refuse to take it." Many of them lost their apartments, got their cars repossessed or sat in the dark because they wouldn't work. Take what you can get until you can find something better. It is not always about what you make but how long you can make it.

# PATIENCE IS VIRTUE

Many times in the working world philosophies change while we're caught in the middle. Shall we leave the company because we were asked to step down? Shall we abandon ship or stay and roll with the punches? I suggest you stay if you can and cooperate to the fullest just to find out if the new direction is the *right* direction. I believe you will fair better down the road because you have a foundation with the company. Remember, no matter how special you are, you can always be replaced. Nature itself replaces its own and you are a part of nature, after all.

# Moderation in Traveling Abroad

When you travel, especially internationally, don't try to do too much in a day. You will never do it all. It's OK to save some points of interest for the next trip. Savor the sites; do not rush from place to place. You will enjoy your vacation so much sweeter. If you get too excited, you will need a week's vacation from your original vacation just to calm down and return to reality.

*Passion For Life, Reason To Live*

# Money Hungry

In the course of life, people are forever money hungry. All money is not good money. In passion for life the reason to live. We should always have options. In my opinion your best option is your own intellectual property that comes from your imagination. A simple drawing in a nice frame will sell. Your artwork does not have to be good. It needs to be good to you. You are the icon. Your dream makes the difference. I recommend you read small business opportunities for entrepreneurs and home base jobs. People have asked me this question. How can I make fast money legally? It is finding the demand for whatever you have to offer.

# IN NEED?

A little girl had a dream. She saw a tall man wearing a white with a peaceful voice that she did not recognize. The voice told her that in two weeks, she was going to get sick and to go straight to the hospital. In two weeks she got sick and walked to the hospital and told the doctor that she was sick. The nurse just thought she wanted attention but the doctor ran a blood test. The girl's white blood cells were producing more than the red blood cells and she needed an operation. She was saved. God contacts his children in mysterious ways because he loves them and wants the best for them in this life.

# AFFIRMATIVE ACTION

Are we going to roll back to a time when there was no hope? Are we going to allow our multicultural population to be polarized with no future? America leads the free world as caretakers for all citizens. A government is not a business with limited goals, it must always provide the hope of opportunity and affirmative action for all citizens. I hope that you will stand with me in support of this cause.

# GUIDELINES OF DEVELOPMENT

- Be a leader. Show the importance of purpose being a vortex of creativity.
- Give yourself plenty of time for contemplation.
- Keep a journal.
- Create a to-do list. Everything counts.
- Post your calendar. Share it with someone.
- Listen.
- Exercise and read. Ward off stress.
- Read stories in time and nature of growth and faith.
- After you save your time, apply your imagination and save your life.

## COMMON STRESSORS

- Not being where you want to be, *where ever that is*.
- Not knowing where you stand emotionally, spiritually or financially.
- Not honoring you priority list of action.
- Procrastination.
- Drowning in papers to read and reference.
- Not being organized.

What good is anything if you can't get to it or you don't know that it is there? I want to help people who share my problems of organization.

# Silver Boxes

Once there was this young lady who lived a sound and moral life. She eventually died and passed into heaven. While in heaven, she stood in a white room with three doors. One door opened while the other seemed locked for good. She asked God if she could peer in the room behind the closed door. He agreed. He opened the door and in the room a thousand silver boxes appeared. Her eyes lit up with curiosity and excitement. She asked what would possibly be in each one. God said that inside were thousands of things that the woman could have had but never asked for.

Do not limit yourself by not asking for what you want. Ask for it and allow the universe to present those gift boxes to you.

# I Know What's Going to Happen

A little boy lay across the bed laughing while reading a book. His father passed the bedroom and he heard the boy taunting, "You are going to get it! You are really going to get it!" The father walked into his son's room and inquired, "Son, I heard you yelling 'you are going to get it' but you are only halfway through your book. What is that about?"

The boy kicked up his feet and lifted his head from the book. "Dad, I began reading this book and already the bad guy was beating up on the good one. I did not like this, so I stopped reading it and skipped to the last chapter. In the end, the good guy destroyed the bad one and got the girl. So now when I read it again, I know what is going to happen. That is why I said to the bad guy when he punched the good, 'That's OK this time because you are going to get it!'"

# What Do You Believe?

The problem with people is that they don't know who they are, what their purpose is or what to believe. Who you are is what God meant for you to be. Whether it's male or female, the responsibilities associated with that identity is your purpose. Look at your history to determine what your historical talents are for your people. Your purpose lies in your dream of what you always wanted to do. This is the focus of your creativity and God's plan for you. Either to be the star of creativity or the producer of the star and lead.

What are you to believe? First, you must believe in a higher authority. Then have faith in yourself to have the cornerstone of judgment for you to know what is right and what is wrong. Knowing what is right and what is wrong is the foundation of judgment. Then you truly know what to believe. As you discover and hold fast to your beliefs, do not get bogged down by the mental stressors that are sure to strike.

# Apply Imagination

You can't get your life back if you can't take the time to apply your imagination to develop the concepts of how you want life to truly be. You have to get to the point of being able to reflect so you can apply your mind. If you are not organized your state of mind will be cluttered and you cannot think as effectively. This is why I wrote this book to help those who need this type of instruction.

The ability to know your place in this world is to understand your responsibilities. Only when you know your place can you be effective and harness the power to perform your duties at your station in life.

What is important to me is organization and harmony. A common ground of ideas and a unity of actions to solve basic problems and centering within peace of mind, contentment and fulfilling goals and desires as much as possible. Without this harmony, there is no relationship.

# Pay the Price

What is the price for the best? The thing that concerns me the most is what you could have had. Maybe with a little more thought and patience you could have had the best of what you want. You force yourself in that rut or tiring situation. It's an inferior product. Due to the feelings you have towards yourself or what category you allow people to place you in, you become that inferior product. You buy into the hype. Get victorious. Determine you own level of achievement by your own skills and talents.

This is one theory that has prevailed in my life. My grandmother had said it: "Always pay for your pleasure." Don't expect free fun. When you pay the price of the ticket the experience is yours for a lifetime. The challenge is not wasting your money; have the right knowledge to know where to invest. My suggestion is to invest with people who have what you want. Fair exchange is no robbery. Entertainers deserve to be paid for the joy they give.

# Labor of Love

Following your dream sometimes may just be a labor of love. Ten years ago, I produced a community-based radio show. I felt there should be an informative talk show to promote local businesses for a nominal cost. All I asked for was a small donation to help assist the production house. I received a few donations and a temporary endorsement for five months. I never, ever came close to breaking even, unfortunately. However, I enjoyed what I was doing and I continued the project until I could no longer afford it. This was my labor of love. Even though it was a financial loss and I never got the support I felt I deserved, I believe I'm a better person for taking on the project. Follow your dream, whatever it is, but do not undermine your financial base while doing it.

*R. Lee Walker*

# Ode to Norman and His Eighty-four Years

1) *Learn something about everything. Then learn about something. Then you won't just be ready; you'll be prepared for whatever will happen.*
2) *Keep moving—you forget about your condition.*
3) *Be in the race so you won't go to sleep on yourself*
4) *On the road of life, construction is never finished.*
5) *Age is mind over matter. If you don't mind, it does not matter.*
6) *Life shrinks and expands in proportion to your courage.*

Thank you, Norman.

# Sunshine

Sunshine, you mean so much to my life.
I look forward to you each day.
I got to be in bed early just to see you rise.
I never know what the day may bring.
Sunshine, I love you.
You are such a part of my life.
I know you realize how special you are to me.
But you have been special to those like me for
billions of years.
Sunshine, you are my life that brings joy.
But for others I know within your sunshine
it has always been death and you continue to rise.
The beauty of it all is where I place myself in the rays
of your love.
God is in sunshine but He is not sunshine.
He is in the nature of your calling but God is not nature.
Sunshine, you belong to yourself and have simple judgments.
I wish you were all mine that I could claim but I share you.
I share your bright gifts.

# A Quality Relationship

The golden rule of a relationship is to have someone you know who is satisfying. It is difficult to be satisfied and not want something more. However, as vanity has no true value, carefully consider what type of person will fulfill you in intimacy. This treasure is something valuable that you find; it does not come to you. Your experience builds who you are.

You look at vanities and I look at true values. You look at how *fly* a person appears and I look at the treasure chest of the heart. Vanities have no substance but the treasure chest overflows with marvelous gifts. It is filled with diamonds, rubies…luminescent emeralds. These gems are *experiences*. And encapsulating every experience is Christ.

The focal point of concentrated optimism representing the highs and lows of man is Christ. Through Him we see redemption and salvation of ourselves. Only through serving a God that you can't see can you open up the channels of creativity and bring out the best in you. Having a material focus in an inadequate object will limit your focus and distract your mind from building your achievements. The mind of God is prolific and universal.

# Philosophy

Life is like a flowing river. It follows in a direction and it has power. The current may be strong or weak; it depends on where the river is at the time and season. We live within the perimeter of the river. We are allowing choices as long as we remain within the perimeter, conscious and receptive. Like fish if they go too high, we get cut off from the Source and die. If we go too low in it, we hit a rock and die. If you have life it all ends in death sooner or later but not at the same place of inception. Our calling is to have purpose and to leave a moral connection. Even though every fish dies, the strength of the river continues because it has purpose for the life surrounding it.

Many people are flashy and deceptive, not offering anything but the superficial self. What decent, wise person will support or pursue such a bad deal or poor risk, connecting to that superficiality? *Ensure your own development.*

# Staying Focus

Watch what happens when you become focused. You must be diligent. You won't have enough time to get it done without interruptions and interferences.

When you set out on executing a project, without commitment procrastination sets in. Then after a while you forget about your project and it will not get done. You have to remain faithful to that idea and the physical manifestation of it. Keep it forever in your mind by keeping it in front of you. Don't wait until the weekend. It won't come.

# Don't Accept Negativity

What good is your efforts if you have no self-esteem and buy into defeat when God promised victory? What happens when you pursue arrogant people and accept what the negativity says when he is a liar? Nothing I say will have true meaning because of what you believe. Negativity will short-change you and strip you of your rights in every area. You will never get ahead unless you say, "I accept the victory that God has for me." You will miss it. The way you are now is not how you will remain. So be careful how you treat people.

Your negative attitude degrades the person willing to pay for your time with love, dedication and compassion. A negative attitude will make you a future basket case headed down the road to personal frustration and disappointment. Negativity will cause you to lose time and money which is the same thing; if you can't get it or simply won't get it, you are not worth the investment.

# Broken Heart

Like many couples, they met in high school. Robert and Dawn got accepted into the same college, scheduled all their classes together and thrived on making plans for the future. Marriage bonded them even further and they moved into their ideal home. They adored that house, raised a beautiful family and cared for pets there. Memories were abundant. Later, they retired and their life together changed forever. They lived on a fixed income, as neither could lift a hand enough to work. Property taxes increased as their health declined. Eventually, they could not afford their home. Refusing to leave, they were forced out by the tax assessor. Before they could carry the last box out the door, they died from a broken heart.

*Passion For Life, Reason To Live*

# TO BE A SUCCESS

Sunbathing next to a pool, a young man admired the gentleman on the next lounge chair. He thought him to be very successful from the confidence in his face and the gold on his wrists. He asked the man what it took to be a success. The man stood up abruptly and pushed the other into the pool. Then he jumped into the pool and began forcing the young man under water. He raised him up, then dunked him a second time. The boy popped up, gasping for air. The man then dunked him again harder. The boy then fought for his life aggressively. Finally, the man stopped this madness. With a beet red face, the young man inquired, "Why did you do that to me?"

The man candidly said, "You asked me what it took to be successful. Well, it takes the same passion you used in fighting for your air to fight for your dream in order to be successful."

# Use Your Faith

There once was a man who owned a boat. This boat took him everywhere. He kept the boat painted, cleaned and decorated. He managed the cargo on the boat. Everything on the boat was in place where it belonged. Then one day a storm came. The sky was so gray it threatened to destroy the boat, drown the worker and kill the captain. The captain managed his boat but he could do nothing about the storm. He was helpless. He knew the storm hovered over his life or death.

Your body is a boat and the storm is stress. It can kill you. Stress causes everything to go wrong. This captain was a special captain because he brought Jesus aboard. The story goes: Jesus was sleeping in the lower desk. Captain woke Jesus and explained what was going on. Jesus went to the front of the ship and addressed the storm, "Be still." And it was done. By bringing Jesus aboard the ship and using faith to call Him up when the stress is too much, you work toward banishing the storm. He will change how you look at it, and provide you with an escape so your boat won't sink.

# INDEPENDENCE

Years ago, my grandfather told me a story. He said there was a man who owned a kingdom and had a son with a deformity. His son was burdened with a hump on his back like a basketball, but he wanted to be treated like a normal kid. So he attended normal classes. Children can be so cruel and they made fun of him. But the young boy maintained a positive attitude anyway. Normally children with that type of tumor don't live too long. The father loved his son and there was nothing he would not do for him. On his son's birthday, he asked what he wanted. His son said he wanted a statue of a Roman soldier with his shirt off, standing straight and tall. The father bought that statue and for twenty years each morning, the son stared at it. Then one morning a loud explosion thundered behind his bedroom door, and blood could be seen seeping through the crack. The father rushed in. The statue was broken in the corner of the room. The father said son where are you? Are you alright? The boy said yes dad I'm fine. I'm over here. What happened? The boy said I was brushing my teeth and something came behind me and struck me with a pin. Then my shirt got wet and I took it off and my hump was gone, then I smash the Roman soldier. Why did you do that? The young boy, now a man, stood straight and tall with no hump in his back. He said, "Daddy, I don't need the statue anymore. Now I'm that Roman soldier."

Who are you aligning yourself with in character and attitude? Will you be somebody's Roman soldier?

# Connection

Think positive and put God first. Simplify your life. Travel to low-cost escapes. Purge files. Get rid of clutter. Spend time in nature. Have a home closer to nature rather than shops and restaurants. Change the floor plan in your home to reflect relaxation. Don't befriend vain people. Life is forever difficult. You will never have enough time to study the problems or enough money to budget. Being in the rat race of life and having to fight to maintain mental balance to stay afloat must be reconciled with love and peace. God specializes in making things right. He rewards us with health and perseverance to endure. Your giving to a worthy cause sets you free from the bondage the system that will put you under. By supporting good causes you should feel a sense of relief by making the world a better place. This will make you feel better about yourself to pull you out of the dumps. By developing higher priorities and better judgment in what you do makes your immediate world a better place to live in.

# FITTING IN

Connecting and not feeling left out is a daily vitamin. Not "missing the train" or wondering where millions of people are is essential to not feeling alone. This is a continuous challenge. Let's get to the bottom of the problem. If there is turmoil in your life, still be mindful of connecting. Without peace you will miss the opportunity to fit in. You judgment will be off center. Fitting in is a window of opportunity and if you stand by yourself, you will miss it.

Once you find the window of opportunity, how long will it last? Fitting in is a state of mind for you and others around you. Others might say you fit in because of your appearance. However, you might not fit in because of how you personally feel. *I don't have the education others have. I can't afford to do the things my friends do. I do not feel loved enough.* We can go on forever with reasons you don't fit in—your own reasons or the ones that others cite.

Perhaps it's time you stop and get a hold of yourself and start practicing contentment with who you are. Slow down and let the world evolve around you instead of you evolving around *it*. You will then become the center of your own energy. You will become a vortex of power to control your life actions.

# Vortexes Field of Energy

There is an area in Arizona called Sedona, which is known for its vortexes. The vortexes are red rock areas containing mass energy below the surface of capped mountains. This energy spins our planet and its force field. Everything that has ever come to being has been called to existence through this field. This field is the field of creativity. It is energy behind the blades of grass. The calling of winter and creation of this planet. You are a part of this force. You are a vortex of good energy. When you promote creativity and bring the best in humanity around you. This is your calling and your purpose.

Life is a process of perpetual motion in fast moving times, it is better to be liquid instead of rigid. The face of your circumstances are changing from the moment of comprehension. You must change your perspective as you access the changing nexus of time. Change your attitude and you change the meaning of the elements that make up the components of your perspective.

# EXISTENCE

Your life is the length of your relationship to the material, physical and spiritual world around you. Your mental condition and the condition of your existence lets you know you are alive. It is important to establish your state of being.

Being is the present. The existence in the changing nexus in time that contributes to the now. Our relationship to the changes in time constitutes stages of importance that require attention.

When you deal with people, what kind of testimony comes from the relationship? Is it good or bad? How do you feel about yourself?

Factors outside of ourselves are responsible for our existence. The air outside of ourselves, the water outside of ourselves. The action of our parents and the calling of God outside of ourselves. Therefore, support God's church by tithing and donate your being to universities of higher learning. Within the universities are the secrets to God's creation.

# Better Than You

A young track star pounded the pavement several hours a day to practice. He could outrun everyone in the school and the state league. One evening while practicing he stopped and yelled, "I love myself! I am the greatest. I know it. You know it. Everybody knows it!" Then an older gentleman standing by the fence said, "I heard you say that you're the greatest so why not take a challenge?"

The track star replied, "You can't beat me, old man. Don't even think about it." The old man huffed and said, "I did not say I could beat you but I can keep up with you. If I can't I'll buy you a new pair of shoes." The track star agreed to the challenge. They went to the blocks then began chanting, "On your mark, get set... go!" The star shot out immediately but it took the older man a little time to get moving. Then something happened. The old man swept by him like lightening and beat the young boy all the way around the track.

The boy scoffed. "How did you do that?"

"That's how I win every time. Just being me."

"Then you are really the champ, not me!" exclaimed the "star."

"No, you're still the champ. I'm not in the contest. There's always someone better than you that you may not know about."

# LOOKING FOR FREEDOM

Every morning at 6:00 a.m. a soldier would walk in front of the same barracks and turn over three trash cans. Then he would pick up each piece of paper, throw it down and shout, "This is not it!" The commander's wife watched him each day and finally told her husband. "Note on the calendar when he does it," said the commander. He hoped to establish some sort of pattern then question the soldier about it.

She watched the soldier turn over these cans for six months, all the while hearing him shout, "This is not it!" She finally reasoned that he was crazy from the stress of war. One morning, the commander did not go to his office. He watched the solider turn over the cans and scream the same mantra. The commander thought to himself that the soldier had serious problems, and it would not be cost-effective to deal with him. A week later, he called the solider into his office and closed the door behind him. His only words: "You are discharged," after handing him a pink slip of paper.

The soldier took the piece of paper and scanned it intently. He calmly said "This is it," then walked out.

# Microwave Popcorn

Almost everyone has popped microwave popcorn at one time or another. You put the bag in and set the timer for three minutes. And wait. Some kernels pop to their fullest after only thirty seconds. Some pop for sixty seconds. Many pop for a minute and a half. At two minutes, only a handful can be heard popping. At the bottom of the bag, once open, you find that a few stubbornly did not pop at all.

It is with emotional maturity that people pop. The circumstance is the heat, the kernels are the people, the timer is the life clock. People mature at different times.

# IMPROVING YOUR POSITION

When you realize you can run instead of walk, you are higher. When you realize you have a ticket to ride instead of hitchhike, you are higher. When you can reduce your taxes to Uncle Sam by giving to the church, you are higher. When you hear the Word and you change your bad habits, you are higher. You will increase your quality of life. And in God, you earn the victory. Stand and give God the praise. If you believe it and accept it, you got it.

# Intellectual Property

*No matter what you have been taught, go after and fight for your dream.* Have you heard the story about the last pearl in the cornfield and the passing traveler who wanted to buy it? This story is in for an update. Let's say a person wanted to buy it. The customer asked the merchant what the cost would be. "How much you got?" fires the merchant.

"I have exactly $12,000." The merchant quickly barks, "That is not enough. Do you own a house?" The customer nods, yes. "I'll take it!" the merchant continues. "Do you own a car?" The customer nods, yes. "I'll take it, along with the house and money." The merchant then asks the customer if he has a wife and kids. The customer hesitates to answer, but nods yes. "I'll take them too for the pearl." Finally, the customer scowls with concern. "If you take them, what will I have left?"

The merchant stands so poised. "I want your heart, body, soul and mind. Everything! Because if you give me everything to get what I have for you, in the end your reward will be a hundred times greater."

By following your pursue in creativity, the source for all rewards, your accomplishments in the quest for intellectual property will be worth the final cost of all your efforts.

# Don't Be Judgmental

A nice boy named Roger raced his tiny motorboat about a mile off shore. Then he saw a leak in the engine and smelled the fuel. The motor spewed black oil and the smell almost suffocated him. He felt something horrible would happen. He ran to the front of the boat, and everything exploded. Roger clung to a splintery board left from the boat. Almost immediately a yacht sped towards him. Roger spotted a man wearing white pants and holding a martini. The light scenario was almost too surreal, too chipper for Roger, who had just lost his boat. As he peered closer, he could see three naked women alongside the captain. Roger thought of the yacht being a den of sin.

The yacht pulled up and the captain shouted, "Buddy, come aboard and let us help you!" Roger paused. He had been raised Baptist and believed that his faith would rescue him, not a boat filled with heathens. "I can't wait on you forever. Are you staying or coming with us?"

"No, I'll be fine God willing."

Then came a helicopter to rescue him. The soldier started letting the ladder down and said, "Young man come aboard."

Roger looked at the helicopter and the soldiers with their machine guns then said, "No thank you, I'll be fine."

The soldier said alright but the water is going to get colder. The helicopter left then a U boat came speeding in his direction. The boat stopped in front of him and one of the men with a Spanish accent had a marijuana cigarette in his hand with a gun said young man come aboard. Roger said no. The boat left and later the water got so cold Roger died. Later he woke up in heaven and met God. He said thank you God I made it, but why didn't you help me in the ocean. God said I did three times, but you did not know me.

# Silver Cloud

Once there was a farmer who lived on a big ranch alone with his son. Their business was to raise horses and harvest corn. One day while the farmer meandered around the field, his son was thrown off a horse and broke his back. A neighbor asked the farmer how he felt about the incident. The farmer dryly replied, "It may be good or it may be bad... I don't know."

That next year a heavy rain came while his son lay sick in bed not able to care for himself. The old farmer could not harvest the crops and tend to his son at the same time. The neighbor next door saw this and said to the farmer, "What are you going to do? Your son can't help you. How do you feel about it?" The farmer said dryly, "It may be good, it may be bad... I don't know." Days later, the farmer lost most of his crops, his very income. The farm was in pure decline. His son was still sick and he had no help. The neighbor next door saw this and asked the farmer how he felt. The farmer said, "It may be good, it may be bad... I don't know."

The following year, the Great War dawned. It required all the young men in the county to go to battle. The neighbor next door came to the farmer and asked him about it. The old farmer said, "It may be good or it may be bad... I don't know."

During the war, the neighbor's son was killed. The next year the war was over and the old farmer's son was up on his feet walking around and assisting his father on the farm. The neighbor asked how he felt. The old farmer said, "It may be good, it may be bad, I don't know."

You never know how what seems like a bad moment may be turned to a blessing later in life.

# BIG MAMA TABLE

Once there was this pretty young woman whose husband died, leaving her to raise three children. She had two girls and one boy. All three children had babies right after graduating from high school. Everyone lived in the same house. Five years later, the children and grandchildren moved out. Fifteen years later, these grandchildren birthed even more children. Now the Mama was known as "Big Mama." Family reunions could no longer be hosted at Big Mama's house, so she structured these celebrations in the local park.

One of the youngest children met a new playmate in the sandbox. When it came time for dinner, the child told her playmate that she had to go eat and would no longer be able to build sand houses. The playmate responded, "I'm hungry too, but I can't go home." The grandchild frowned. "Don't worry. Come to the table. It will be very crowded, so Big Mama won't recognize you from the other children in our family."

The little girl had been right. Big Mama looked at her and smiled as if she were one of her own. Unlike Big Mama, you cannot fool God. You won't be able to sneak by him and set at his table because he is going to know you.

# Good Night, I'll See You In the Morning

A dying grandmother called all of her children and grandchildren to be with her. She knew she had only one week to live. At night she called them to her bedside and said, "Good night, I'll see you in the morning." She said that to all five except one. To him, she said, "Goodbye my son." She stated this repeatedly for almost a week until the son replied, "Mama, why do you say, 'Good night, I'll see you in the morning' to everybody else except me? I love you too."

Grandmother sighed. "I know you love me but the way you are living your life, if I died tonight where I'm going, you will never be because of the life you are living. So honey, it will have to be goodbye. If you love me, you will have to change your ways and come to Christ."

The boy smiled brightly in wonder. "Mama, I do love you and I will change my ways and come to Christ."

"Then my son, let me say to you good night, I'll see you in the morning."

# Resolution

People in stressful situations look for opportunities and a way out of the turmoil. The next level is taking action and calling on God to help you. Don't bow your heads in shame. Stretch your arms out, close your eyes and look up to God and call out for help.

An important forum is conflict resolution. This subject is avoided in many schools and institutions. What do you do? Well, how far have you treaded into the relationship? What is your timeline? How much time do you have to live considering twenty years as twilight time? I believe if you can't work out the issues you should use the wedge of time to diffuse the emotions. Your commitment remains to your responsibilities but your presence is not effective there until the environment is right. You have to remove yourself from that situation.

People have problems when they lose God. When you lose God, you lose love. When you lose love, you lose respect. Without respect people don't have compassion and become bloodthirsty.

# In Our Hearts

Once there was a single mom with three children. It was tough to make ends meet but they kept a beautiful, comfortable apartment. In the evening, their mother scampered into the kitchen while the children played with their goldfish and watched television. One evening, the children's grandmother came for a visit. After kissing the children, she hurried into the kitchen to help her daughter prepare fried chicken, biscuits and corn. Within minutes, a scream filled the house. The grandmother told her daughter that she would handle the commotion, assuming one of the children fell or hit another. All three were actually found crying over the fish bowl.

"Our fish is floating! It's not breathing. Help it, Grandma!" one shouted. With one quick motion, the woman pulled the fish out with a tissue and left the room. She told her daughter to continue cooking, then entered the living room to console the children. "Kids, your fish is not dead. She is still alive in your hearts. Just remember all the fun times, tricks and swims she gave you. She did it to make you laugh. What I took outside is only her shell." The children believed their trusted and wise grandmother. They stopped crying at once.

Years later, their dear grandmother passed away. All three children sat in the front row of the ceremony as the family minister stepped to the podium. "We have come to honor a terrific lady. Though she is dead... " Before the minister could finish, the woman's grandson jumped up abruptly. "You're a liar, preacher!" Everyone turned to the boy in shock. "That's right," the boy continued with passion. "My grandmother is not dead! That's just a shell in that casket. She is alive in our hearts forever, just like our goldfish."

# Children Learn From Parents

The tidy home included three children, a mother, father, and a well-respected grandfather. As soon as the grandfather retired, he was considered no longer useful; therefore, the children asked him to leave the house and sleep in the barn. The adult son gave his father a horse blanket while the little ones watched. Sadly, the grandfather stayed in that barn until his last breath. Years later, the child who witnessed him leave the house grew up and had kids of his own. At this time, his father lived with the family so everyone could begin the process of caring for him.

Soon, the son called him to the kitchen table. "Father, I want to talk to you. It's nice to have you around but it's time for you to go." Flabbergasted, the father buried his head in his hands. "But it's cold out there, rainy and lonely," he pleaded.

In reply, the son gently handed him a horse blanket. "This will keep you warm. It is the same one you gave to Grandpa. Please... go." Children learn from their parents. Never doubt that they are not always alert, watching and taking after you.

# Shipwreck

The sailor loved mornings best but today was different. A thick fog poured over the horizon and into his path, steering him away from his usual jaunt. His ship crashed in the back of a deserted island. It remained afloat but another problem festered. Wild animals surrounded the ship, so the man stayed hidden for a week. Unfortunately, his food ran out. He turned to coconut juice to quench his thirst and his hunger. After years of sailing, he could not believe the predicament he landed in. He prayed to God.

Amidst exhaustion, the man lay on shore, not caring if the animals tore him to pieces at this point. He smelled smoke. Right before his eyes, the ship exploded. "Oh God, I have nothing!" he screamed in anguish. Within minutes, a boat sped toward him from under the horizon. The captain called out to the sailor. "Are you all right? Do you need medical attention?"

"How did you find me? I've been here for days... days! And no one has come." The captain claimed that he saw an SOS smoke signal, so he did not hesitate to respond. As the sailor began to cry, the captain assured him, "God's help always comes. You are not alone, you are not alone, my friend."

# The Box

A mother had punished her five-year-old daughter for wasting a roll of expensive gold wrapping paper. Money was tight and she became even more upset when the child pasted the gold paper so as to decorate a box to place under the Christmas tree. Nevertheless, the little girl brought the gift box to her mother the next morning and said, "This is for you, Mama." The mother was embarrassed by her earlier overreaction, but her anger flared again when she found the box empty. She spoke in a harsh manner: "Don't you know, young lady, when you give someone a present there should be something inside the package?" The little girl looked up with tears in her eyes, urging, "Oh Mama, it's not empty. I blew kisses into it until it was completely full." The mother was crushed. She fell on her knees and put her arms around her little girl. She begged for forgiveness for her unnecessary anger.

An accident took the life of her only child a short time later and it is still told that the mother kept that gold box by her bedside for her remaining years. Whenever she faced difficult problems she would open the box and take out an imaginary kiss, remembering the love of the child who had it there.

In a sense, each of us, as human beings, have given a golden box filled with unconditional love from our children, family, friends and God. There is no more precious possession anyone could hold.

R. Lee Walker

# It's Not About You

The governor and his wife were traveling in a long black limousine enroute to a speaking engagement. The driver panicked, as he was completely lost; however, he did not have the courage to notify the prominent couple. He drove fast, searching for a gas station all the while hoping that the couple would not notice his anxiety. No gas station was in sight. He turned off the main road to explore the area. The car traveled nearly ten miles until they approached a small, run down station on the side of a dirt road. Hoping to reach a bathroom, the driver hurriedly exited the car before the couple could object.

An old attendant walked around the limousine, inspecting the tires and hood. His suspenders and jeans shook off specks of dirt every time he moved slightly. With snow white hair and thick whiskers, it was unclear how clean the man really was. The governor watched his every move. Finally, he spoke to his wife: "Honey, doesn't he look awful familiar?" She agreed. The thought occurred to him finally. "Honey, I recognize him. He is your old boyfriend." The woman peered closer, recognizing him at once. "You're right, I can't believe it's him. What's he doing in a place like this?"

The governor chuckled with delight. "Do you realize that if you would have married him, you would have been in a place like this?" Just then, the woman broke his hold on her and insisted: "No, no, you're wrong! If you would not have married me, you would have been in this place."

# Mantra

How will you know what to believe if you don't know the difference between right and wrong? How will you establish justice? Without justice you will turn everything around; the good will be bad and the bad will be good. True value cannot then be established. The result will be poor choices. You will misuse the righteous and miss the golden opportunity of discovery because you won't know what you really want.

It is not right for you to know everything or understand everything. Knowing too much brings sorrow. God makes everything but everything is not for you. God is good because He gives you a mind to understand what you need to survive.

I see God in *uniformity* and *consistency*. Uniformity and consistency are indicative of a pattern of thought and do not merge by chance of happenstance. Only through divine need and purpose is anything created. Chance and randomness do not possess the power to *create*.

Life is our relation in a moving nexus of time to the physical objects around us. Our life in God is an independent gift for us to cherish. We are allowed to make our own choices. For Him to make our choices would be against the purpose of development. Life in the highest order is the quest of discovery amidst the enigma of motion. We learn by doing. God does not search for knowledge because God is not a man. God made nature; He is not of nature. God made the air and water, but He does not serve as the substance life is made of even though he dwells within it. He gives everything to you but He won't live your life for you.

The challenge is finding the purpose for your life. God will inform you; He will send a supreme message in your spirit. What bothers you the most in life? This is your reason to live. Live to do something about what you see you don't like. You must take action in believing.

Do you know what to believe in? If you don't know what to believe, you won't understand what you should act on. Then you will make the wrong choices and miss opportunities. Your frustration will push you to transform the right into bad and the bad into good. You will then lose sight of the goal and purpose you were put here for in the first place. In this life you will only know so much. You have to tap into your innate creativity, the place inside that propels you to think uniquely and deploy. Do not take this intuition for granted. For instance, you look at one sun and one moon. There is one sun in our galaxy but there are billions of suns throughout the universes. Our world like a grain of sand lying in the desert. But God is the same God in all these worlds.

Everything we do points us in the direction of having core values. Without the ability to recognize the truth you won't know true value. You will waste precious time in vain circumstances that hold no worth. In this state, you place yourself in bondage behind worthless pursuits that will not bring you true joy and lasting peace. Once you know true value you will be free of the world of worthless results.

Why does God present obstacles and negativity while you undertake the challenge of discovering your purpose? The greater the challenge the greater the opportunity for success and sheer victory.

An important tool is the surroundings you keep. Your association and counsel should be with the righteous because they will influence your judgment and what you believe. Those who are not righteous do not care about your greater purpose; they will divert you from your goals through their own selfish interests.

One day, I asked a man on the streets what was the worst thing he had ever done. He did not tell tales about robbing banks or murdering someone. He insisted when he had lost faith in God he lost faith in himself. When he lost his faith he lost his hope for the future. Without hope for tomorrow and faith that you can get there, there is no goal and no reason to live.

The most important thing for us is our faith in God. Within this faith harbors our worship, positive attitude and generosity. All these components will take us to a better place in the Lord and in our life. We will underestand better what to believe by our experience through personal knowledge and our understanding between right and wrong.

# New Life Today

New life is the life we create for ourselves. You can have life today, free from guilt of the past and fears of the future. In forgiveness of the past refer to Romans 5:8: "God demonstrated His love towards us, in that while we were yet sinners, Christ died for us." In strength for today, refer to Ephesians 3:20: "God is able to do exceedingly abundant things above all that we ask or think." In confidence for the future, refer to John 5:24: Jesus Christ promises that everyone who trusts in Him has "everlasting life and shall not come into condemnation but pass from death unto life." This means nothing if you don't believe.

Does my written concept inspire you to think on issues of religious thought and to generate decisions? Why am I here, you ask? I am here as a philosophical religious writer. I am here to inspire the collective.

Changing your mindset is the positive reflection of time and commitment. By being disciplined, you won't have to face bankruptcy and deprivation. Based on your political and social affiliations, you will have a defense fortress. You must establish yourself outside of a system of corruption and self-absorption. Labor is definitely a resource of financial support, opportunity, growth, development and confidence, friendship, desires, spiritual strength, and conquest. You must avoid conflict and litigation by being effective and invisible, then pursue what you want. Your new life is built on what you know and what you want to change.

# Count Your Blessings

In high school at recess, people used to come to the fence and beg for food. We knew they did not have money. Sure, some deceived and pretended to be poor but many of them had not eaten in days most likely. A little boy stumbled upon a crowd, wanting to hear a sermon. He asked his mother for a fish sandwich. What was going through his mind when the man of the hour asked for his sandwich and he knew Jesus had more than anybody? This was a test of faith. It's not about your money. Heed anonymous words because we are so fortunate:

If you woke up this morning with more health than illness, you are more blessed than the million who will not survive this week.

If you have never experienced the dangers of battle, the loneliness of imprisonment, the agony of torture, or the pangs of starvation, you are ahead of 500 million people in the world.

If you can attend a church meeting without fear of harassment, arrest, torture or death, you are more blessed than three billion people in the world.

If you have food in the refrigerator, clothes on your back, a roof overhead and a place to sleep, you are richer than 75 percent of this world.

If you have money in the bank, in your wallet and spare change in a dish somewhere, you are among the top 8 percent of the world's wealthy.

If your parents are still alive and still married, you are very rare, even in the United States.

If you hold up your head with a smile on your face and are truly thankful, you are blessed because the majority can but most do not.

If you can hold someone's hand, hug them or even touch them on the shoulder, you are blessed because you can offer God's healing touch.

If you can read this message, you just received a double blessing in that someone was thinking of you and furthermore, you are more blessed than two billion people in the world that cannot read at all.

Someone shared these words with me.

# Personal Assassination

Personal assassination can be deadlier than a bullet. A bullet will kill you quickly. The steel into your flesh and the trama, you are dead. Personal assassination will kill your influence and you will live to feel the pain. How many years will it take to heal? I've seen it happen so many times. Don't let anyone kill your influence.

Once there was a sergeant who became a lieutenant. He had taken a job nobody wanted him to have. Due to the jealousy in his department individual officers were told not to listen to him and conduct business as usual. Upper management would not consult with him and he was never advised of current policy changes. He was kept in the dark and reprimanded for not having leadership qualities. His influence was killed and he had no power. Nobody would listen to him.

Even in my own family, as a child I witnessed this happen to my grandmother in church. She had been an avid churchgoer. The more money she paid to the church, the more responsibility she received. She could be seen with the microphone every Sunday. My grandmother enjoyed testifying and having the microphone. When the day came when she could no longer deliver those special messages, the microphone was given to someone else. Then rumors got started about her and the pastor of the church. Now her testimony was tainted and her influence destroyed, even though the rumors were not true.

The moral: Policies change just like the wind. Don't let anyone kill your influence. Continue to be committed to your cause. If you stop in the face of criticism, you validate the false statements and negative allegations. No matter what others say about you, remain dedicated and determined to what you believe.

# Encourage Yourself

You never know how blessed you are until tragedy strikes. So don't ever tell me you are bored. For as long as you can do for yourself you should be thankful to God. How often do we let opportunities slip away, and shout, "I wish I would have done that!"? There is no certainty that you are going to wake up in the morning.

Being placed on the road of life with all its challenges is a gift within itself. The opportunity to participate and enjoy its rewards and failures within a culture of involvement is a gift to be thankful for. The option of choice is a gift. A man once said, "I'm having a bad day but I'm thankful for having a bad day to have." There are people who wish they had energy to look forward to another day or moment.

# ENCYCLOPEDIA OF WISDOM

*by Anonymous*

You will never remember the total story I tell you. Take what you can from it and use it. You can never pay me back; pass the knowledge to the next generation.

Say less and repeat less.

The world could have listened to Jesus when he was twelve. He had to get a little older. Pay me now or pay me later for your mistakes.

Everybody has a story to tell. Listen and learn.

Everybody is here to discover and learn. We can learn from each other.

I want to feed you and let you go free, free to learn from your choices. Having freedom of choice is the beauty of it all. Knowing you have the choice is the understanding of it all.

Moses wanted to reach back and strike the rod the same as before. Things change. People change, moods change, and circumstance change.

Make the transition from imagination to faith. To know in your spirit what you believe already exist.

Pursue teachers that offer solid rocks in judgment and emotional growth who improve your decision making in the choices in life that you select. Be with those who help you balance judgment and equity in legal affairs in rendering justice for all.

Run with artists and writers who help you explore your imagination. This is the fullness of life.

Challenges are worthwhile if the goal is worthwhile.

Think of Thanksgiving every morning. Giving thanks yields more thanks. Keep an optimistic outlook.

Care about your health. A positive attitude translates into a higher state of being, which yields better choices and peace.

Praise exceeds criticism four times.

Recharge your spiritual, mental and physical batteries.

Go beyond the normal.

Spend time thanking a family member or a friend.

Gratitude involves sharing, appreciation and growth.

Well-traveled people open your eyes to certain human behavior. They aspire to greater wisdom and greater understanding of how the world works.

Work is what you do, not who you are.

Now is the time to enjoy and attain what you can.

People get tired of the same thing.

Your test of leadership could be the battle within your relationship.

Don't try to measure your worth with people who don't inspire you.

Time searches out and destroys all things.

The earth is in motion in God's will. The laws of right action promote total creation and development.

If you want a better understanding about human behavior, be with people who shed enlightenment on understanding.

You will never realize the true value of what you are offering in service if the people do not want it.

The more words you know, the more ideas you can entertain.

The more you know, the better protected you are.

# MAKE DREAMS COME TRUE

Encourage yourself.

Avoid negative people, places, things and habits.

Believe in yourself.

Consider things from every angle.

Don't give up and don't give in.

Enjoy life. Yesterday's gone. Tomorrow may never come!

Family and friends are hidden treasures. Seek them and enjoy their riches.

Give more than you planned.

Hang on to your dreams.

Ignore those words that question you.

Just do it!

Keep trying no matter how hard it seems. It will get easier!

Love yourself at first.

Never lie, cheat or steal. Always strike a fair deal.

Open your eyes and see things as they really are.

Practice makes perfect.

Quitters never win and winners never quit.

Read and learn about everything important to you.

Stop procrastinating!

Take control of your destiny.

Understand yourself in order to better understand others.

Visualize your dreams.

Want your dreams more than anything.

Accelerate your efforts to make your dream come true.

Fear is not only pain. We operate in the pain or pleasure syndrome. We sharpen our skills in pain and learn better in peace and pleasure.

# Patience

A little girl named Carlie adored money. In fact, even though she couldn't count very well yet, she watched her mother write deposit slips, count change, roll dollar bills, and fill out bills every day. She finally asked her mother if she could go to the bank with her. "Carlie, banks are boring, they're not for kids." But the girl begged. "Mommy, I'll be quiet. Please, just let me see the bank."

The mother gave in. She always did eventually, as Carlie was her only child and very spoiled. Both approached the teller, who immediately took to the child and offered candy from the jar sitting on the counter. "They're all kinds. Tootsie rolls, gummy worms, suckers. Have whatever you want." When Carlie did not make a move towards the jar, the teller put her own hand in. She retrieved a few pieces and gave it to the child. "Thank you, Miss," she said shyly.

The following week, Carlie returned to the bank with her mother. "Would you like some candy?" the same teller asked. She tried to hand the entire jar again to Carlie, who did not respond. Giggling, the teller chose a few random pieces and handed them to her. She nodded in gratitude then stepped back. The next week, the same thing happened with the teller offering Carlie the jar then eventually the candy. Her mother sat her down once they returned home. "Carlie, why won't you get the candies when the nice teller offers them to you?"

"It's simple. If I grab the candy, I can only get so many. When she does it, she grabs more because her hands are large!"

God's hands are bigger than yours. Wait on His blessings, which will be more than you can handle.

# The Last Supper
## by Anonymous

"The Last Supper" was painted by Leonardo Da Vinci, a noted Italian artist, and the time engaged for its completion was seven years. The figures representing the twelve Apostles and Christ himself were painted from living persons. The life model for the painting of the figure of Jesus was chosen first.

When it was decided that Da Vinci would paint this great picture, hundreds of young men were carefully viewed in an endeavor to find a face and personality exhibiting innocence and beauty, free from the scars and signs of dissipation caused by sin. Finally, after weeks of laborious searching, a young man nineteen years of age was selected as a model for the portrayal of Christ.

For six months, Da Vinci worked on the reproduction of this leading character in his famous painting. During the next six years, Da Vinci continued his labors on this sublime work of art. One by one, fitting persons were chosen to represent each of the eleven Apostles. Space would be left for the painting of the figure representing Judas Iscariot as the final task of this masterpiece. This was the Apostle, you remember, who betrayed his Lord for thirty pieces of silver worth $16.96 in our present-day currency.

For weeks, Da Vinci searched for a man with a hard, callous face with a countenance marked by avarice, deceit, hypocrisy, and crime; a face that would delineate a character, who would betray his best friend. After many discouraging experiences in searching for the type of person required to represent Judas, word came to Da Vinci that a man whose appearance fully met his requirements had been found in a dungeon in Rome, sentenced to die for a life of crime and murder.

Da Vinci made the trip to Rome at once, and this man was brought out from his imprisonment in the dungeon and led out into the light of the sun. There, Da Vinci saw before him a dark, swarthy man; his long, shaggy hair sprawled over his face, which displayed a man of viciousness and ruin. At last, the famous painter had found the person he wanted to represent the character of Judas in his painting.

By special permission from the king, this prisoner was carried to Milan, where the picture was being painted. For months he sat before Da Vinci at appointed hours each day, as the gifted artist continued his task of transmitting to his painting this base character in the picture representing the betrayer of our savior. As he finished his last stroke, he turned to the guards and said, "I have finished. You may take the prisoner away."

As the guards were leading their prisoner away, he suddenly broke loose from their control and rushed up to Da Vinci, crying, "Oh Da Vinci, look at me! Do you know who I am?" Da Vinci, with the trained eyes of an artist and student carefully scrutinized the man upon whose face he had constantly gazed at for six months and replied, "No, I had never seen you in my life until you were brought before me out of the dungeon in Rome." Then lifting his eyes toward heaven, the prisoner said, "Oh God, have I fallen so low?" Then turning toward the painter, he cried, "Leonardo Da Vinci, look at me again, for I am the same man as the figure of Christ."

Many lessons can be learned from this true story of the painting of "The Last Supper." This is a story of how we often perceive others, how easily we overlook the Christ within the people we meet and judge by outward appearances. This also strongly teaches the lesson of the effects of right or wrong thinking on the life of an individual. Here was a young man whose character was so pure and unspoiled by the sins of the world, that he presented countenance of innocence and beauty fit to be used for the painting of a representation of Christ. But within seven years, following the thoughts of sin and a life of crime, he was changed into a perfect picture of the most traitorous character ever known in the history of the world.

# God's Door

The steps of a righteous person are doing the right things. Listen to that inner voice that might save your life and your integrity. Pray and read your Bible. Be a doer of the Word.

Refer to Proverbs 11:11 and 28:19: "He that tilleth his land shall be satisfied with it." Proverbs 13:20: "Walk with wise men." Epistle of John 1:11: "Follow not which is evil, but that which is good. He that doeth good is of God, but he that doeth evil hath not seen God."

We need to learn to praise the Lord as much for a closed door as we do an open door. The reason God closes doors is because He has not prepared anything over there for us. If He didn't close the wrong door, we would never find the right door. God directs our path through the closing and opening of doors. One door closes; it forces you to change your course. Another door closes; it forces you to change your course again. Then finally, you find the open door and walk right into your blessings! The Lord directs our paths through the opening and closing of doors but instead of praising Him for the closed door (keeping out of serious trouble), we get upset because we judge by appearances. You have an ever-present help in the time of need, who always stands guard. Because He walks ahead of you, He can spot trouble down the road and set up a road block or detour accordingly. But through our lack of wisdom, we try to tear down the road blocks or push aside the detour sign.

The minute we get into trouble, we cry, "Lord! How could you have done this to me?" We have got to realize that the closed door can be a blessing. Didn't He say that "no good thing will He withhold from them that love Him?"

If you get terminated from your job, praise God for the new opportunities that will manifest themselves. It might be another job, it might be school. If that man or woman won't return your call it might not be them; it might be the Lord setting up a roadblock. Just let it go.

One time a person called upon their bank to grant them a loan of $10,000. The person had been tied to this bank for years. The Lord urged their spirit to call another bank. That bank gave them $40,000 at a lower interest rate than the first bank was offering! We can sometimes trap ourselves in doubt and discouragement through judging by appearances.

I'm so grateful for the many times our Heavenly Father has closed doors to me just to open them in the most unexpected places. The Lord won't always say in spoken words, "Go to the left, now to the right." Sometimes, He will just close the wrong doors. "Thy Word is a lamp unto my feet and a light unto my path," says Psalm 119:105. "The steps of a good man are ordered by the Lord and He delights in his way," continues Psalm 37:23. And "The mountain top is glorious but it is in the valley that I will grow! For the Lord is good; His mercy is everlasting and His truth endureth to all generations," proclaims Psalm 100:5.

The passages in here taken from the King James version of the Bible.

*Passion For Life, Reason To Live*

# Honoring Billy Graham

People ask why I was put here. They can't find happiness in their life. I remember visiting rich movie stars like Gloria Swanson, who made more money than other women could dream of having. They tried to find fulfillment in sex, cars and other "things." They had not found it because they did not have God in their lives. They had material idol gods.

Scientists are mystified because new galaxies are being formed before their very eyes every time they look. What powers are creating the new galaxies like new babies being born? Only God can create galaxies, and they are witnessing His handy work.

*I drove into a small town and a man asked what the death ratio was. The man pumping the gas said, "One to one. " Everybody has' to give an account of everything they've done on this earth. If you break one of the Ten Commandments, you may have broken them all You can't expect to be perfect and walk the walk without the Holy Scripture to assist you.*

Now there are more scientists going to church and believing in God more than ever before. They always knew there were billions of stars. Now they know there are billions behind the billions they already knew about. God is on the planet as a spirit. He has no sense of time. He is the same yesterday as He is today. Mr. Graham proclaimed: "The problems that we have are race problems because the heart of man is sinful. It started a long time ago in the Garden with the first man and the first woman. Adam and Eve were told not to eat of the tree of consciousness and if they did, everything would change. They ate of the tree and brought sin into the world.

Just like there is a judgment side to God, there is also a forgiving side to God. God is love. There is so much love that He gave His only begotten son so that you may live. Jesus died for your sins. On the cross, Jesus said, "My God, why has thou forsaken me?" God hates sin and Jesus became sin and God did not want to look at him.

*From the time you are born, time already starts drawing near when you must return back to the Father. Are you going to be ready? You will never know the hour or the moment when it is your time to go. Friend, you need Jesus in your life. Be saved. He is the only way. Come now and accept Him as your personal savior and I will pray with you.*

(Notes from Billy Graham sermon"

# My Sermon

We know that God allows diversity. People are allowed to do whatever they want. So the big question is why evildoers are so prosperous and seem to have so much, and God's people in the church are so poor. You want to admire the back stabber with big houses on Palm Beach and in the Caribbean with large fleets of cars. You think they made it and they don't go to church. Material things don't bring happiness. A big house with lonely rooms that are cold with no friends, family and visitors is not happiness. Being scared behind locked gates in a big mansion with cameras and guns to protect your life with no freedom to come and go is not happiness.

Just being able to come to church in sound mind and ask God what you want with others doing the same thing in peace and unity is success in itself. You are victorious over the wicked just to be here today. Psalm 37 is the answer.

People commit suicide and they seem to have everything. Yeah, they did everything before they died except God. When seeking God for answers you have something to look forward to. You can apply your faith, increase hope and believe in your heart that there will be a better tomorrow in God because he saves. Where else can you find this much inspiration?

Sharing represents humankind's highest order. Just to be able to share is indicative of a state of higher being. So, give whenever and where ever you can. A tremendous problem in the world is covetousness or selfishness (wanting more than what is rightfully yours). To act on it causes confusion. This is corruption. This unwise person who does not want to do what is right, generates this discord. Through their own deception they lie to themselves wanting to keep everything and everybody under their own lock and key.

Through love and friendship, you can attract people to you if they themselves want to be righteous and in sync. Sin is buried in the heart of humanity. It is up to us to root it out by our desire to want to do the right thing within our own lives, which could also mean facing the truth about our own faults.

"He went too far and stayed too long, and gave too much to the wrong type of person." Adultery happens when you overwhelm yourself in your selfish desires and deny your responsibilities. Fornication happens when you deny what you know to be true and go along with what is wrong and think that is okay. It is important to have drive because you develop know how as you practice. Excess materialism will destroy your life. I saw a movie where a Coke bottle dropped from heaven and landed amidst an African tribe. Everyone wanted the bottle and stumbled over each other to get to it. This bottle destroyed the community.

Your titles say to God, "I'm not buying into excessive consumption or materialism. I don't need another pair of shoes or shirt. I'm satisfied." I want to support the spirit of light, the spirit of creativity. What you give to God comes right back to you in energy and mental good will. You are edified in worship and praise. Less money for less materialism and more money toward praise and worship will build your life. There will be less clutter, more simplicity and better decision-making, which in turn, will improve your life and further help you reach your goals. You're shedding defeat, selfishness and greed. It propels you to your highest form of existence. God knows this. Tithing is for you. Our job is to protect and preserve God's creations.

# FAITH

Let me tell you a story about Paul and Joy. Paul met Joy while they were in college. Paul used to see Joy running down the sidewalk, rushing to a political science class every other afternoon. Finally one day, he stopped her to ask her out. She quickly accepted and took his phone number, then trotted off as usual. Within a few months, they had fallen madly in love. They both graduated that year and worked side by side to purchase their first home. Soon, Joy was pregnant.

The day came when her water broke and Paul rushed her to the emergency room. Everything seemed fine until the doctor ushered Paul into his office. Paul did not waste a moment. "What's wrong, doctor? Is Joy all right? Where's the baby?"

"Paul, I hate to tell you this but your wife will die if she has the baby. If we abort the baby, she will live to have another one. What do you want us to do?" Paul's head spun. He was in denial that there even would be a problem considering that there had been no problems during Joy's pregnancy. She had not even experienced morning sickness. Paul walked out of the room in a complete daze. He entered the nearest supply closet and got down on his knees. "God, what do I do? I want a son, but I love my wife. I would do anything for her." Paul waited and God did not answer. In tears, Paul went back to the doctor.

"Doctor, I've left it up to God. Please do what you can for both of them. Joy is strong. God gave me my wife and she is carrying my son that God gave us." The doctor left at once and delivered the baby. All the while, Paul had not left the doctor's office. He sat in the chair with his eyes focused on God's will, God's power, God's love for him and his family.

When the doctor came in with the announcement, Paul was beside himself with happiness. "Now Paul, I told you it would be a difficult delivery. She's lost a lot of blood but several nurses are administering to her right away. I believe she is going to be fine. You were right, Paul, you were right to trust in Him."

# Never Give Up

There was a single mom who worked in a hotel as a maid. She believed in paying her tithes faithfully. She had a son who loved to play basketball. The coach used to tell her son that he was a good player and he would surely progress over the years. Her son Dre was not good enough to play varsity but be could play B classification The coach predicted that be just needed some special attention before being able to move into varsity status. So the coach told Dre that the gym would be open on Monday nights between 5:00 and 7:00 for him to practice in. The following Monday, an assistant coach was scheduled to meet Dre for one-on-one training.

Dre waited and waited, but no one showed up. He waited the entire two hours. The next day, Dre approached the coach and expressed his disappointment. The coach apologized incessantly and swore that someone would be there the following Monday to show him all the awesome shots. That person did not show again. Finally, the coach promised to be there himself.

To Dre's dismay, his trusted head coach did not appear. Sitting on the bench exhausted from disappointment, Dre could not understand why be had been lied to in this manner. Dre made up his mind to practice alone the next time. That day he had shown up at exactly 5:00, and pumped the basketball into the hoop before the clock struck 5:01. Soon, Dre had gained momentum and with a fury, the ball made it through the hoop nine out of every ten times.

Suddenly, he heard another bounce loud on the gymnasium floor. It came from the rear of the gym from the opposite end of the court, where a man towered over. The ball drilled through the hoop in jet time. Again and again. Dre was amazed at this spectacle across the gymnasium. What kind of athlete could this possibly be, Dre mused. His routine symbolized sheer perfection. In one quick motion, the man seemed to spring across the floor near Dre. "Who are you?" he stammered. The man said, "Michael." It wasn't that Dre didn't really know who this man was; he just did not think it possible to really be having a conversation with him just inches away, sharing the same sport. "You are... Michael?" The man snickered. "Yes, Michael Jordan, that's me and only me."

Michael stayed with Dre the rest of the evening, teaching him over one hundred tricks. The greatest trick of all? Believing in himself. When Dre bounced through the door and greeted his mother, the power of his happy entrance swayed her back to the couch. "Son, what happened?" But his beaming smile said all she needed to know. Dre said "Guess what happened to me today?"

# MONEY CAN'T BUY PEACE

There was once a rich man, a CEO of a major corporation. He made $800 million per year. He was so powerful, he didn't look at anyone. He looked right through everyone. He refused to talk to anyone; he talked at them. Nobody mattered except competing CEOs or family members. He gave his family the best of everything. Then one day while talking on the telephone, he experienced a sharp pain in his right side. So he called his doctor for an appointment. Later that afternoon he left in his limousine to go to the doctor's office. The doctor performed normal tests. He tapped his knee, then used the stethoscope to check his heart. The doctor examined his chest, then his back. The he said, "Chuck, I would like to take x-rays of your heart. In fact, I insist on it."

Chuck complied. How could he not? Afterward, the doctor reviewed the results and turned to Chuck. "Chuck, I am going to be frank with you. You need a new heart. The heart bank is empty and we will have to get one from a private donor." In a flash, Chuck's life was in turmoil. From that day on, he was restless, discontent and frightened. He had no semblance of peace within.

After two weeks passed, he told the doctor he would personally pay $10,000 more for the heart. Two more weeks passed and there was no response. Chuck told the doctor to increase the cost to $50,000 more. No one answered so he doubled the amount. Then one evening a couple walked into his hospital room. They asked if he was the man who needed the heart. "Yes, please help me," Chuck whispered.

"A few years ago, you destroyed my son's life with a stroke of your selfish pen. You fired him. I'm dying right now too, but I would not give you my heart for no amount of money, the man spat. You superficial idiot, you will rot for the pain you've caused so many people because all you cared about was a title. Rot in hell!" With that, the man gently grabbed his wife's hand and led her out of the room, quietly closing the door behind them. Chuck was flabbergasted his money could not buy the man's heart. He had no idea who the man's son might have been, as there were so many over the years. Sheer desperation flooded him.

Chuck was in so much turmoil until the doctor brought in a roommate named "Willie." Willie's space was overcrowded with laughing visitors and flowers that had been sent virtually on a daily basis. After visitors left one evening, Chuck asked Willie why he was so calm about waiting on something as important as a heart. Willie smiled and said, "All my life I treated people the way I wanted to be treated. I never intentionally misused anybody. God has been so good to me I always worked for everything I've gotten. I have no regrets in life. If I get a new heart, fine. If I don't I'll be just as satisfied. I will die in peace."

Chuck didn't say a word. He felt anxious and uncertain what his future held, if he even had a future. Neither one received a heart. Chuck died in turmoil and Willie died in a peaceful sleep.

Which person are you? The rich man, who thinks his riches will be his salvation, or Willie, who tried hard to be kind and loving?

# Communication

Once there was a young boy who lived in a luxurious apartment. He enjoyed sports and taping events on his VCR. One day the machine would not record, so he took it to a local repair shop. The man checked the machine, huffing and puffing the entire time as if be was exasperated to even work in the first place. After checking the equipment, he threw up his hands and urged the boy to buy another VCR. The boy did not say a word. All he could think about was missing another evening in front of the television with his favorite games and movies.

First thing in the morning, the boy headed to a different electronics store to purchase a new VCR. "Do you have anything cheap but effective?" The salesperson scowled and chuckled. "That's absurd. You want quality but you don't want to spend money?" When the boy didn't respond, the woman led him to a vast selection. "Pick your brand." The young man only tried two and chose the first one. He took it home.

The boy planted the machine exactly where the other had sat. He handled the remote, trying a variety of buttons. The screen displayed a cloudy blue square. He pressed "play" at least twenty times before hurling the machine against the floor. The machine looked exactly like the old one.

The salesperson was not happy to see him again. "This is damaged goods and you took my money yesterday. Here's the VCR. Where's my money?" the boy's voice grew louder with frustration. "Did you read the manual? Did you carefully review the menu?" she asked flatly. The boy had not but did not want to admit it.

I tell you this story because the only ending it needs is this: Reading a manual is like listening to the other person. You can't know how to relate without listening, so how would you know how to operate the relationship to get the desired results. Just because people look alike that does not mean they are the same.

# Paid in Full

*by Anonymous*

Is the packaging important to you? A young man was getting ready to graduate from college. For many months he had admired a beautiful sports car in a dealer's showroom. Even through the cold, frosty glass, he could see every patch of the automobile, every reflection. He finally told his father that for graduation, he would be so content to have this car, nothing else... ever. As graduation approached, the young man was certain his rich father would purchase the car.

An hour after the big celebration, his father beamed with delight before handing him a small package. Surely this had to be the keys, the boy thought. He unwrapped the silver paper and stared at the gift in disbelief. "With all your money, you give me a Bible?" the boy screamed breathlessly. He stormed out of the house, leaving the Bible on the kitchen table among champagne flutes, cake and balloons.

Many years passed and the young man had become very successful in business. He had a beautiful home and wonderful family but realized his father was very old. He thought perhaps he should go to him and apologize for what he had done in the past. He had not seen him since that graduation day. Before he could make arrangements, he received a telegram stating that his father had passed away. The man had left everything to his son, who was summoned home to make the funeral arrangements.

The first thing he did was attempt to find the Bible. Within minutes, he found it in his father's locked box under bills and gold coins. With tears, he opened the Bible and turned the pages. His father had carefully underlined a verse, Matthew 7:1 "And if ye, being evil, know how to give good gifts to your children, how much more shall your Heavenly Father which is in heaven, give to those who ask him?"

As he read those words, a car key dropped from the back of the Bible. It had a tag with a dealer's name, the same one that harbored the cherished sports car years before. On the tag was the date of his graduation and the words, PAID IN FULL.

How many times do we miss God's blessings because they are not packaged as we expected? Don't you know that the best gifts are always hidden from view?

# Four Wives

*by Anonymous*

Once upon a time, a rich king kept four wives. He loved the fourth wife the most. To show his adoration, he draped her with rich robes and treated her to the finest of delicacies. She knew nothing but the best of every armchair, piece of jewelry, toiletry and plate of food. As for the third, the king luxuriated in showing her off to other dignitaries because she emanated such beauty and charm. However, he feared that she would eventually leave him for another.

He loved his second wife for her confidence, kindness and patience. Whenever the king faced a problem, he would confide in her, as she would help him get through difficult times without judgment or pause.

The king's first wife made a very loyal partner. Business-savvy and intelligent, she offered great contributions to the maintenance of his wealth and kingdom. However, the king did not love her nor did he express any feelings whatsoever towards all her generous gifts. Sadly, she loved him deeply.

One morning, the king fell ill and he realized his time would be short from this hour on. He thought of his luxurious life and wondered, "I now have four wives with me but when I die, I'll be alone."

Thus, he asked his fourth wife: "I have loved you the most, endowed you with the finest things and showered great care over you. Now that I'm dying, how far will you follow me and keep me company?"

"I'll follow no where!" replied the wife, "When dead you are gone," and she walked away without another word. Her answer cut like a sharp knife right into his heart. The sad king then asked the third wife, "I have loved you all my life. Now that I'm dying, how far will you follow and keep me company?"

"I'll follow you to the church." Replied the third wife. "Life is too good! When you die, I'm going to remarry!" His heart sank and turned cold.

He then asked his second wife, "I have always turned to you for help. You've always been there when I needed you. When I die, will you follow me and keep me company?"

"I'm sorry, I can't help you out this time!" replied the second wife. "At the very most, I can only walk you to your grave." Her answer struck him like a bolt of lightening and the king was devastated.

Then a voice called out, I'll go with you. I'll follow you no matter where you go." The king looked up and there stood his first wife. Suffering from malnutrition and neglect, her skinny frame edged closer to the king. Extremely grieved, the king shouted, "I should have taken much better care of you when I had the chance!"

In reality, we all have the four wives in our lives; the fourth and most sacred is our body. No matter how much time and effort we lavish in making it look good it will leave us when we die. Our third wife is our possessions, status and wealth. When we die, it will go to others. Our second wife is our family and friends. No matter how much they have been there for us, the longest they remain by our side is until the grave.

Finally, our first wife is our Soul. Often neglected in pursuit of wealth, power and pleasures of the world, it is the only companion that will follow us where ever we go. Cultivate, strengthen and cherish it now, for it is the only part of us that will follow to the throne of God and continue with us throughout eternity.

# HE WILL ANSWER PERSONAL QUESTIONS

I rented a house owned by my mother. I wanted to move but before I moved I wanted to ask for God's advice. I prayed to God and discussed my situation. The answer came within three days. I worked downtown as an accountant and frequented Persian Square. I decided to feed the birds. A sweet elder woman sat down beside me on the bench, striking conversation before the birds devoured the last bread crumbs. She said, "I wish my husband and I bought that old house."

"Excuse me?" I responded politely. "Yes, young man," she said. "I wish we would have bought that old house. It would have been worth a fortune today! My husband and I felt that we were too young and did not want to be tied down with unnecessary responsibilities. We could get up and move when we were ready without any problems. We wanted this freedom. Our friends bought an old house, sold it for a large profit, then settled in by the ocean," she explained.

I listened closely, as her words seemed so familiar. "The last time I heard, they sold their ocean-side house in Oregon and moved to a bigger house, which they paid cash for. As for us now, we can barely afford the apartment we live in. The rent keeps increasing!" The woman's story was my first confirmation.

The next confirmation struck at a 76 Station in Beverly Hills. I pulled into the self-service island. While I prepared to pump the gas, a black attendant strolled over to offer assistance. I obliged and handed him the pump. He began talking about his mother's old house that no one wanted to fix up or live in. The decrepit walls were apparently days away from caving in and the floor sank with age. It needed paint and the plumbing had failed weeks before. When his mother tried to sell it to him so she could settle into a retirement community, he had declined like everyone else. The house finally sold for a meager amount. The new owner repaired everything in no time, and the "old" house was now worth one hundred times the cash he had given for it.

The last confirmation was in the Sunday morning paper, where the main headline read, *Home Prices Are Going to Soar.* I received the final message, and I'm glad I did. My $30,000 house boasts a $600,000 price tag today.

Listen to strangers. God speaks through them in your time of question.

# THE SHINY ONE

### by Anonymous

Arlene wondered if she was supposed to connect with this strange man. There was nothing on the ground except a single darkened penny and a few cigarette butts. Still, her companion had reached down and picked up the penny. He held it up and smiled, then put it in his pocket as if he had found a diamond ring. *How absurd*, Arlene thought. What need did this man have for a single penny? Why would he even take the time to deliberately pick it up?

Throughout dinner, the entire scene nagged at her. Finally, she could stand it no longer. She casually mentioned that her daughter once kept a coin collection and asked if the penny he had pocketed represented some value. A smile crept across his face as he reached in and dug the penny out for her to see... again. She had seen and spent so many pennies before. What was the point of this?

"Look at it," the man insisted. "Read what it says."

"United States of America," she recited.

"No, not that; read further."

"One cent?" she haughtily replied. He shook his head patiently.

"In God we trust?"

"Yes, yes!" he shouted. Arlene frowned. "And?" she pressed. "And if I trust in God, the name of God is holy, even on a coin," her date continued. "Whenever I find a coin I see that inscription. It is written on every single United States coin but we never seem to notice it! God drops a message right in front of me telling me to trust Him? Who am I to pass it by? When I see a coin, I pray. I stop to see if my trust is in God at that moment. I pick the coin up as a response to God. For a short time, I cherish it as if it were gold. I think it is God's way of starting a conversation with me. Lucky for me, God is patient and pennies are plentiful!"

Arlene smiled politely but did not say much more during dinner. The day after, she found a penny on the sidewalk during a shopping trip. She stopped and picked it up. In that instant, she realized that she had been fretting about things she could not change. She read the words, "In God We Trust." She laughed. *Yes, God I got your message.*

Thereafter, Arlene found an inordinate number of pennies for months. Then again, pennies are plentiful! And God is patient.

# MIXED RELATIONS

Once there was this middleclass family that dedicated all their attention to the oldest daughter. She had fallen in love with a young man who had pursued her for months with flowers at their doorstep, theatre tickets, singing telegrams and the like. Her father finally asked her why she had not invited him to meet the family. She did not hesitate to make arrangements for dinner at their home.

The next day she invited the young man over. When she introduced him to her father with an expectant smile, everyone noticed a mole above his right eye just like the father's. He asked the young man, "Who is your mother?" The boy replied, "Janice Thomas."

"Oh, Janice Thomas? Well, what is her maiden name, if you don't mind me asking?"

"Janice Shaw."

The father responded, "Janice Shaw was my classmate, what a coincidence." Then he left and approached his wife in the kitchen. He immediately told her that he used to date the boy's mother. "As a matter of fact, she was my girlfriend for some time. I loved her..." His voice trailed off and the room grew eerily silent.

"Are you saying that young man may be your son?" she inquired.

"Yes, it's possible. I heard she was pregnant after we parted but she would not see me to discuss the situation. Do not tell our daughter she may be dating her brother! Let's just discourage her from seeing him again after dinner. We must..."

After a few weeks, the daughter became fed up with her parents' insistence that this boy was not right for her. She finally cornered her mother, who admitted that her father thought she might be related. Stunned, the daughter shouted, "I love him! How could this be?"

"Sweetheart, continue to date him in spite of your father."

"Why, Mama?"

The woman sighed long and hard before responding, "The reason is that boy is not your brother because your *dad* is not your father."

# How to Write a Book and Avoid Being Money Hungry

Everyone always ask me how to write a book and I never have time to answer. So in this short conversation I intent to answer how I wrote My first book. I what to give you the steps you need to take to make it Happen.

First you must know your passion. What is it that you want to talk about? What concerns you the most? What story do you want to tell? Once you figured that out, it is time to start your research. How long will it take for you to develop enough information to have a viable product? For me it took 27 years to write a simple poetry book. My notes were lying around in envelopes and hanging on my wall for years. Part of the problem I did know how to do it. I did know how to get published and the other problem was procrastination. How about being lazy.

For you to get started I suggest you buy yourself a loose leaf note book Then count out lease a hundred and twenty pages Within those pages You write what ever comes to your mind until you fill up the entire book. I tell you this because within those pages is passion. Without passion you have no substance and your book won't sale. Once you completed your assignment now it is time to edit your ideas. This is what you build on. What are the main points? What is the main theme? What is your Hook for your book? The real assignment starts now. Rewrite your book with the questions I mentioned in mind. Rewrite your book, then let it rest for a week. Reread it and rewrite again if necessary. Do a spell check on the computer or review your hand manuscript. I don't like writing on a computer unless I back up my material. I can't afford to lose anything. The next step is to find you a good editor.

That could be a problem. I have paid editors that don't do the work. Look at them like independent contractors. Get an estimate and pay in increments until the job is done.

Next find at least five people to review your work. Pay them for their opinions. If too many questions pop up about your work. You did not do your job well. The less questions the better the work. Resolve all questions. Get the final review.

Next bring closure to your writing. Sometimes you will be writing forever Always revising your book and you will never get it right. Ask yourself this question. If had only a year to live what would be the most important things to say? Say it then stop. Keep I mind fiction and nonfiction are different. To me nonfiction is easier to write. For example poetry and personal stories. However fiction is a world of its own. You have to Write it, sleep with it, marry it, cultivate it, nurture it, to develop it until it is ready to leave on it's own. I rewrote my first fiction book thirteen times. To me it is a commitment. Once it is done a big job is over. Congratulate yourself.

Next copy writes your product by sending it back to yourself through U.S. mail and certain writer's registries. Send your product to a book publisher or do it yourself through self-publishing. Join a marketing association to help you market your product. What I did not mention is you need to find yourself a printer and a graphic designer if you self publish. Believe me that is a job within itself. Go to the library and find a book on the self-publishing that we will further assist you. Once you have went through all the steps you have to sell your product personally to through any bookstore you can find. It becomes a question of motivation and determination to get your money back. Let as many people know about your product as possible. Use gorilla marketing tactic by just walking up to people and showing your product. That is the best way through word of mouth.

I just want to give you some highlight and a general preview on what you are in for to write a book. To write and publish a book is a lot of work and it does not come easy. It involves a commitment and a lot of personal time and energy, money, and dedication. I want you

## Passion For Life, Reason To Live

to know that most successful books are failures. Even though a book is on the best sellers list as number One, it does not mean that it has recaptured it's cost. So don't expect to a lot Of money at first.

It may take years to get your money back for the time you invested. You may not get it back at all. Maybe your children will reap you rewards. To write should not be about the money but the passion. I like the attention I get. This is something where I can get full credit for my work. It is something that will last for two hundred years after I'm gone. Finally find people and authors who are doing what you are doing. This way you can share information and help each other. There is lot of information to know. And I just wanted to share some of my ideas on how I got started. Good luck

Finally I want mention a few jobs that people never talk about:
- Copy Write Editor. This is a person who read material for the final printing.
- Money Broker. This is a person who loans money where it is needed most.
- Research Assistant. This is a person who will do research and verify statements and documents.
- Mediation Coach. Mediators come in all levels of life. People choose the type of person they want to be their mediator.
- Travel Charge Line Consultant. Give advice on areas of the world you travel.
- Personal Cook. You don't have to be a housekeeper, you can just be a personal cook. Cooking is an excellent trade.
- Buy Your Own Printing Press. Everybody needs some type of printing for commercialization.
- Create Your Own Support Club. Whatever it is start a dues paying club to support it. If it is your vision you put yourself in charge.
- Adult Daycare Facilities Are Needed Almost Everywhere. Start one or work in a facility is a good opportunity.
- Personal Readers. Read to people are tell them what you think of their material.

- Marketing Assistant. Hire people to hand out flyers in the community to advertise local businesses.
- Deliver Telephone Books. If you have a small truck have your own delivery service.
- Personal care giver, and personal assistant. You will take care of errands.
- My favorite quick money job, sell your won art near your home. You set the price.

Maintain a smile and positive attitude in what you are doing. Find your market for what ever product you have and you will not be money hungry.

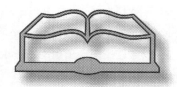

# DISTANT TOURIST

Once there was this young traveler who spent all his money on tours before his vacation was over. He was staying at his last hotel before going home. He was depressed so he went to the lobby just to be in a festival environment, While he was sitting in the lobby a well dress middle age men came up to him and asked him loan him $5 dollars. Young man told him he did not have it. The stranger said I understand. Then he said let's do something about that. Meet me tomorrow on the beach in front of the hotel at 10am. The following morning the young man met the stranger. The stranger said we can do something about being broke. The older man directed the young to go up the board all and collect the color bottle and put them in a box and bring them back. So he went and collect a box of bottle. Now the young man was told to follow him to the edge of the sea canal and there we can find different color shells and rocks, and seaweed. So they left the bottles and took the box to that location. They found different color rocks and shells. They also found the seaweed that they needed. They took the items with them back to the bottle. They clean the bottles with ocean water then they tied the corol seaweed around the rocks and shells. Then they tied the cord to the top of the bottles. They had two rock and two shells around it each bottle. Then the older man told the younger man that they could go to the tourist port where the cruise line arrives. At the cruise port they found a shelf to display the bottles. When tourist arrived one ask how much are the souvenirs. The old man how much do want to pay. The tourist said $15 dollars. The old man said okay. They sold all the bottles. They took that money and bought two fishing poles, bread, wine, wood and a blanket. They cleaned and ate the fish, told jokes for the rest of the evening. The old man told the young man to meet in the lobby the next day. The next day the young man saw his friend in the lobby during happy hour. His friend saw him and smiled. The young boy went to the section of the room where he was but he disappeared. The morale of the story is you can be happy without spending a lot of money. You be happy without spending your money at all.

*Passion For Life, Reason To Live*

# BUILD RELATIONSHIPS

The Lone Ranger and his partner Tanto were being followed out of town by what they thought was a bad guy. Being the good Indian, Tanto could not see the guy so he got off this horse and placed his ear to the ground to hear the galloping of the horse. He tried hard to calculate the distance between them but he still could not see the villain for miles. As the Lone Ranger traveled further, he asked Tanto, "Where is the guy now? Please tell me."

Tanto turned to him and said, "I see him now! Just a dot of him but he's moving. It's him for sure!" The Lone Ranger nodded, having no reason to doubt his friend.

After fifteen minutes, the Lone Ranger asked again, "Where is he now? Please tell me." Tanto shot his head back to check the bad guy's whereabouts. "He's gaining! He's getting bigger, so I can tell he's closer to us." He measured six inches in width between his hands. They rode some more, increasing their speed. The Lone Ranger called out again. "Tanto, where is he now?" Tanto looked back, then measured about a foot. They rode more, tangled in urgency. Within minutes, the Lone Ranger prompted Tanto again. "Where is he now? Surely he's getting closer by the minute."

Tanto did not hesitate. "He's huge! He's right behind us. He's gaining!"

"Shoot! Shoot him, Tanto!" shouted Lone Ranger. Tanto drew his gun but did not pull the trigger. "I can't, I just can't." The Lone Ranger opened his mouth in shock. "Why? Why are you betraying me?"

Tanto looked the Ranger square in the eye. "I've known him too long! Ever since he was this small." And he gestured with his hands.

So you see, people feel differently about you once they get to know you. Their loyalty increases as your time together strengthens. Build relationships.

# GET THE PASSION

If you have an immediate dream you can make the most of my suggestions happen without spending a lot of money. However it is important that you have discipline and you share your dream with like minded people. There is unity with like minded people. There is value and appreciation in ideas when you get where you are going they will be there with you to support you. The passion for life and love is reason to live is knowing what you really want and being allow to pursue it while you can.

# I Just Woke Up I'm Grown

There a woman laying in bed with her husband sleep. Then she woke up and started to stare at the ceiling.

Her husband said "Honey, what is wrong?"

She responded, "I just grew up."

He said "What you mean you just grew up, we been married for ten years pass high school and got three kids."

The morning the husband went to work, but when he returned his wife was gone. There was a note on the bed saying,

*I have been living all my life for other people, and who they thought I should be. For years I have been invisable to myself. Now it is time for me to live for myself.*

When did you wake up to the reality you are your own person?

# The Rose

There was a little boy sitting with his father on a porch holding a rose. The little boy was squeezing the rose and pulling it's petals.
The father said "What are you doing."
The boy said "I'm trying to open the rose like God, but I'm destroying it."
The father said "I know, you see God works on the inside, and when the time is right it will open on its own."

# SPECIAL TREE

There was a man who had a vacant garden in front of his house. For five years he water the same spot waiting for a special Japanese tree to grow. The neighbors did not know why he watered that spot. Finally the tree took root and sprang up from the ground. Passer's by think that the tree was just a normal tree not knowing the years of cultivation.

Talented people don't just arrive overnite.

# The Rich Waiter

There was a young man who worked as a waiter over a low end hotel. He had a very nice atitude and disposition. When he served he food and he always ask his customers what were there hobbies. Then he would listen. If they said art, he would invite them to see his art collection after business hours. He priced his art cheap, but later the word spread. People came to the resturant just to find out about his next art show. As more people came, he raised his prices. His party became so popular until his painting earn enough to buy the resturant below and purchase the building he lived in. Don't give up your dream.

R. Lee Walker

# Knowing the Value of Your Service

Once there was a young boy who could not figure out the value of his service. He said to his father "Can you help me."

The father said "Sure son just a minute."

The father went to a back room and came back with silver coin. The coin had a split down the middle with a man sitting on a stool.

The father said "Son take this coin to the eastside and see what you can get for it."

The boy took the coin to the eastside and stopped at the first shop he saw and went in.

The merchant approached him and said "What can I do for you?"

The boy said "What can I get for this coin?"

The merchant took the coin and held it up in the air and said, "Young man, this coin has no value."

The boy said alright and departed.

Then he went to the second shop on the eastside and talked with the merchant. This very short light voice man said, "Young man this coin is too dull, it has no value."

The boy said alright then departed.

He went to the third shop on the eastside and gave the merchant his coin. The merchant took the coin then held it up in the sky. Then he droped it on the ground, then picked it up again. Then the merchant said, "This coin has no value, but I will throw it away for you."

The boy said, "Throw it away! Give me back my coin!"

Then the boy went back to his father and said "I can't get anything for this coin."

The father said, "Son try the westside."

So the young boy went to the westside and stopped at the first shop he saw. He asked the merchant, "What can I get for this coin?"

The merchant took the coin and looked at it then said, "I'll give you 30 talents of gold, all my furs, and half of my shipment for tomorrow."

The boy said, "What did you say?"

"I'll give you 30 talents of gold, all my furs, and half of my shipment for tomorrow."

He said "I will take it."

So the boy took the gold coins, and the furs and as he was walking out the door he stopped. He said, "Sir, why do you want to give me this?"

The merchant said, "Young man the coin you just exchanged with me is the last minted coin from the great empire of Persia Minor and it is an honor to have it in my collection."

So the boy went back to his father. As he was walking in the door his father had a smile on his face. The father said "My son you did very well for yourself, what have you learn from all of this?"

The boy paused for three seconds then said "Father what I learned from this is, whatever you have to offer, offer it to someone who understands it's value and knows it's worth."

Within this story is the secret of business success, and you will never be money hungry.

# STAYING AHEAD

Maintain a good name and good credit. Borrow money that you can pay back when you don't need it. Get as much as you can and keep it liquid. I suggest cash accounts, gold coins and US Saving Bonds. Save money to have reserve accounts to back up your expense accounts. This is hard to do, but make this your priority goal. You have to stick to your budget. Saving money is your defense in hard times. The key to not being money hungry is to have somewhere to turn for help when you need it. Most important is that you are able to turn to yourself first for the help you need.

# WATCH YOUR COMPLAINING

There was a flock of birds flying south for the winter. One little bird took the lead then when it got tired it dropped back to the rear. While in the rear his wings got cold and began to freeze. The poor little bird tumbled from the sky to the ground on the side of the road. While on the side of the road, an old cow saw him then walked and stood over him and dung all over him. It sure did smell, but it was warm. The little bird stayed in it for quite some time. Now he was tired of the smell and he wanted out. So he started flapping his wings and making loud noises Down the road an old tom cat heard him. The tom cat came over and pulled the little bird out. Then he washed him off. The little bird was happy, then the tom cat smiled at the little bird and ate him. The moral of the story is, just because someone dumps on you does not make them your enemy. Just because someone helps youu, does not make then your friend.

# IT'S YOUR LIFE

There was this young man who was interested in sky diving, So he asked the instructor if he could go up in the airplane and watch his students jump. The instructor agreed. The next day he was ready and there were seven jumpers. They went up to about 20,000 feet. The student opened the door to the aircraft and they all jumped. However, the young man noticed the last jumper's parachute did not open. He ran and told the instuctor. The instructor said, "I'll turn the plane around." While turning the airplane around, the young man slipped out of the airplane without a parachute. The young man saw the other student who's parachute would not open. He was fighting with the cord and hitting himself upside the head and crying. He was making himself sick. While the young man without a parachute said to himself, "I know I'm going to die so I might as well enjoy the view, tumble, and be as free as a bird." The person with the parachute had a miserable life. The man without the parachute had a wonderful life even though it was short. Which person would you rather be?

# THE VALUE OF YOUR WORD

Make an agreement with yourself on what you really want to do with your life. Keep your agreement and honor your word. When you break your word it means that your agreement doesn't matter. Keep your word in life with everybody. Be a responsible person for what you do. Don't play a victim of circumstances. Take a position on what is important.

Write in this book, make this book yours.

A. List five things you want to have in your life, which you do not currently have:

1)

2)

3)

4)

5)

B. What considerations (limiting beliefs) get in the way of being, doing, or having what you want? (For example: I'm not confident enough in myself. I'm not intelligent enough. I don't have enough education. I'm too old/young. My race, my family, etc.) List at least four:

1)

2)

3)

4)

C. Use the space below to describe your dream or vision for your life. What do you really want? Be specific. Again, What do you really want?

*Passion For Life, Reason To Live*

# FORGIVENESS

Who in your life has caused you the most harm. Is it your mother, father, sister, brother, co-worker, ex-lovers, or so-called friends? You are in charge of your life. All choices are up to you and nobody else. Make the choice to forgive now, and move on with your life. List the people you forgive. Then say I forgive you by name.

1. _____
2. _____
3. _____
4. _____
5. _____
6. _____
7. _____
8. _____
9. _____
10. _____

I forgive you now. Don't block your future gift. The worst eternal punishment is knowing what you could have had if only you forgave. Clear your mind of that on going relationship whether they are dead or alive.

# PASSION FOR LIFE
## *JOURNAL*

Day:_____  Date:_____  Time:_____

**What do I want out of life today?** _____
_____
_____

**What is my to do list?** _____
_____
_____

**What affirmations will I speak today?** _____
_____
_____

**What in life can I change to make it better today?**
_____
_____

**What can I give to brighten someone's day?** _____
_____
_____

**What do I remember most about this day?** _____
_____
_____

# PASSION FOR LIFE
## *JOURNAL*

Day:_____ Date:_____ Time:_____

What do I want out of life today? _____
_____
_____
_____

What is my to do list? _____
_____
_____
_____

What affirmations will I speak today? _____
_____
_____
_____

What in life can I change to make it better today?
_____
_____
_____

What can I give to brighten someone's day? ____
_____
_____
_____

What do I remember most about this day? ____
_____
_____
_____

# PASSION FOR LIFE
## *JOURNAL*

Day:_____ Date:_____ Time:_____

**What do I want out of life today?** _____
_____
_____
_____

**What is my to do list?** _____
_____
_____
_____

**What affirmations will I speak today?** _____
_____
_____
_____

**What in life can I change to make it better today?**
_____
_____
_____

**What can I give to brighten someone's day?** ____
_____
_____
_____

**What do I remember most about this day?** _____
_____
_____
_____

# PASSION FOR LIFE
## *JOURNAL*

**Day:_____  Date:_____  Time:_____**

**What do I want out of life today?** _____
_____
_____

**What is my to do list?** _____
_____
_____

**What affirmations will I speak today?** _____
_____
_____

**What in life can I change to make it better today?**
_____
_____

**What can I give to brighten someone's day?** _____
_____
_____

**What do I remember most about this day?** _____
_____
_____

# PASSION FOR LIFE
## *JOURNAL*

Day:_____  Date:_____  Time:_____

What do I want out of life today? _____
_____
_____
_____

What is my to do list? _____
_____
_____
_____

What affirmations will I speak today? _____
_____
_____
_____

What in life can I change to make it better today?
_____
_____
_____

What can I give to brighten someone's day? ____
_____
_____
_____

What do I remember most about this day? _____
_____
_____
_____

# PASSION FOR LIFE
## *JOURNAL*

**Day:** _____ **Date:** _____ **Time:** _____

**What do I want out of life today?** _____
_____
_____

**What is my to do list?** _____
_____
_____

**What affirmations will I speak today?** _____
_____
_____

**What in life can I change to make it better today?**
_____
_____

**What can I give to brighten someone's day?** _____
_____
_____

**What do I remember most about this day?** _____
_____
_____

# PASSION FOR LIFE
## *JOURNAL*

Day:_____ Date:_____ Time:_____

What do I want out of life today? _____
_____
_____

What is my to do list? _____
_____
_____

What affirmations will I speak today? _____
_____
_____

What in life can I change to make it better today?
_____
_____
_____

What can I give to brighten someone's day? _____
_____
_____
_____

What do I remember most about this day? _____
_____
_____
_____

# Conversation with the Author

Q: What is the true meaning behind all your stories?
A: Can you dance?
Q: What do you mean, sure I can dance. I can dance with or without a partner.
A: Not that type of dance, I mean do you know the dance of life! My stories are to build judgement and understanding. Do you understand when to push forward or pull back in any situation? When you acquire wisdom you will know what pursuits are worthwhile. If certain perimeters don't exsist like no communication or the other party won't listen then that is a divided house and it won't stand. Why pursue a situation that you know is goingt to fail. All my stories are design to prepare you for the dance. Remember have a purpose in life, establish goals. Keep in mind these few points:
1. Visualize your goals.
2. Write your vision.
3. Share your vision with like minded people.
4. Stay positive and run from negativity.
5. Have a plan and take action on it.
6. Have a written reason for your goals.
7. Have faith in God and yourself.
8. A fail is success upside down. Make adjustments then try again.

The road in life is always under construction. Life and death is in the power of the tongue, so you create your own future by what you say. If you do and say the right things to the right people, you will never be money hungry. May you forever have joy hyappiness, and peace of mind. God loves you.

R. Lee Walker

# About the Author

R. Lee Walker was born in Prentiss, Mississippi. He moved to Los Angeles, California with his grandparents, Leroy and Alberta Walker. He graduated from California State University – Dominguez Hills. Later, he completed graduate work at the University of California at Los Angeles.

Mr. Walker is a philanthropist and he loves communication and ecology. He has traveled extensively throughout the world and speaks several languages.

He lives in Los Angeles with his family.